She Acts Very Different

by Linda Cundy

tate publishing
CHILDREN'S DIVISION

She Acts Very Different

This title is also available as a Tate Out Loud product.
Visit www.tatepublishing.com for more information.

Published by Tate Publishing & Enterprises, LLC
127 E. Trade Center Terrace | Mustang, Oklahoma 73064 USA
1.888.361.9473 | www.tatepublishing.com

Tate Publishing is committed to excellence in the publishing industry. The company reflects the philosophy established by the founders, based on Psalm 68:11,
"The Lord gave the word and great was the company of those who published it."

Cover and interior design by Elizabeth M. Hawkins
Illustrations by Liz Holt

Published in the United States of America

ISBN: 978-1-61777-907-7
1. Juvenile Nonfiction / Social Issues / Special Needs
2. Juvenile Nonfiction / Religious / Christian / Social Issues
11.10.19

Dedicated to my husband
and children who have
supported me on this
journey with April...

and of course to April.
She is my inspiration.

There is a young girl
I would like you to meet.
Her giggles, her hugs,
and her smiles are a treat.

She loves meeting children,
children like you.
So listen as I tell you
some things she will do.

She likes to play games
little children will play,
like turning the faucet
so water will spray.

She loves to pretend
she is hiding from me,
but she's easy to see
right in front of the tree!

She plays very different;
God says it's okay.
He loves her so much
and likes her this way.

She talks with her hands
to let us all know
she likes Christmas lights,
swimming, and car rides...

Let's go!

When she sees her friends,
she lets out a squeal!
She wants them to know
that her love is real.

She sounds very different;
God says it's okay.
He loves her so much
and likes her this way.

When she sees the marching
bands come down the street,
she's up, and she's clapping,
moving to the beat.

Her run looks so funny
with her hands in the air,
but she's faster than fast,
so she doesn't care!

She moves very different;
God says it's okay.
He loves her so much
and likes her this way.

Shih Tzu

She picks up the puppies
and holds them
TOO TIGHT!
We all try to teach her and
show her what's right.

She taps, and she pulls
to make sure that we see.
I'm here! Over here!
Just please, look at me!

She touches so different;
God says it's okay.
He loves her so much
and likes her this way.

This girl is so good
about showing her joy.
Are you good at that,
little girl, little boy?

She knows about Jesus
and how to show love.
So watch her and learn.
God's watching from above.

There are children like this girl
whom some day you'll meet.
Just talk to them; play with
them; they really are sweet.

They may not do things
that most children do,
but they're important to God
and their families, too.

They act very different;
God says it's okay.
He loves them so much and
likes them this way.

e|LIVE

listen|imagine|view|experience

AUDIO BOOK DOWNLOAD INCLUDED WITH THIS BOOK!

In your hands you hold a complete digital entertainment package. In addition to the paper version, you receive a free download of the audio version of this book. Simply use the code listed below when visiting our website. Once downloaded to your computer, you can listen to the book through your computer's speakers, burn it to an audio CD or save the file to your portable music device (such as Apple's popular iPod) and listen on the go!

How to get your free audio book digital download:

1. Visit www.tatepublishing.com and click on the e|LIVE logo on the home page.
2. Enter the following coupon code:
   ee28-8377-3420-4844-fab3-c125-f879-0f5e
3. Download the audio book from your e|LIVE digital locker and begin enjoying your new digital entertainment package today!